DOMESTIC DOGS

YORKSHIRE TERRIERS

by Susan H. Gray

Published in the United States of America by The Child's World®
PO Box 326 • Chanhassen, MN 55317-0326
800-599-READ • www.childsworld.com

Our thanks to William A. (Bill) Wynne, and Marcia Wynne Deering for their assistance in making this book possible . . . and to Schotzie and Lady for being such cooperative models.

PHOTO CREDITS

© Bill Kennedy/Associated Press: 23
© blickwinkel/Alamy: 19
© iStockphoto.com/Lisa F. Young: 11
© Jack Sullivan/Alamy: 17
© Juniors Bildarchiv/Alamy: 27
© Mary Berendes: 15, 29
© Pat Doyle/Corbis: 21
© tbkmedia.de/Alamy: 9
© William A. Wynne: 25
© Yann Arthus-Bertrand/Corbis: 13

ACKNOWLEDGMENTS

The Child's World®: Mary Berendes, Publishing Director;
Katherine Stevenson, Editor

Content Adviser: Gale A. Williams-Thompson, Public Education Chairman,
Yorkshire Terrier Club of America

The Design Lab: Kathleen Petelinsek, Design and Page Production

LIBRARY OF CONGRESS CATALOGING-IN-PUBLICATION DATA

Gray, Susan Heinrichs.
 Yorkshire terriers / by Susan H. Gray.
     p. cm. — (Domestic dogs)
 Includes bibliographical references and index.
 ISBN 1-59296-778-7 (library bound : alk. paper)
 1. Yorkshire terrier—Juvenile literature. I. Title. II. Series.
 SF429.Y6G73 2007
 636.76—dc22   2006022641

Table of Contents

NAME That DOG!

What small dog came from England? ❧ What dog changes color as it grows older? ❧ What dog picks on other dogs ten times its size? ❧ What dog has the nickname "Yorkie?" ❧ There is only one right answer—the Yorkshire (YORK-shur) terrier.

5

It All Started in Scotland

Before 1870, no one had heard of Yorkshire terriers. But people had other kinds of terriers. Terriers were hunting dogs. Some people in Scotland had "waterside" terriers. These dogs got their name from hunting otters. Otters are animals that live near water. Watersides were small dogs with long, gray coats. People also owned Clydesdale terriers and Old English terriers. These three **breeds** no longer exist today.

Scotland and England are found on the island of Great Britain. The map on the left shows where Great Britain is on Earth. The map on the right shows a closer view.

Atlantic Ocean

Scotland

North Sea

Northern Ireland

Ireland

England

Atlantic Ocean

Wales

Great Britain

English Channel

France

7

Yorkshire County is in northern England. It is not far from Scotland.

Over time, people from Scotland moved to England. Some settled in Yorkshire County. They brought their terriers with them. The different breeds of terriers began to have puppies together. Owners would keep the best-looking babies. When those puppies grew up, they would have babies of their own. In time, these new terriers looked different from the three terrier breeds.

In 1870, someone put one of these terriers in a dog show. A news reporter wrote a story about the dog. He said it should be called a "Yorkshire terrier." The name caught on. Yorkshire terriers are still known by that name today.

Soon, people in America heard about these little dogs. They wanted Yorkshire terriers of their own. Today, "Yorkies" are a **popular** pet. They are one of America's ten most popular dog breeds.

Yorkies are very curious. They like to watch people or other dogs to see what they are doing.

9

Furry Little Toys

Yorkshire terriers are one kind of toy dog. Pugs and some poodles are toy dogs, too.

Yorkshire terriers are small dogs. They are about 10 inches (25 centimeters) tall at the shoulder. They weigh about 7 pounds (3 kilograms). That is less than most house cats. Because of their small size, Yorkies are called "toy" dogs.

These two Yorkies have different haircuts. Do you like the one with longer hair or the one with shorter hair?

Yorkies are little, but they get lots of attention! People love their long, beautiful coats. Some Yorkies' coats even drag on the floor. They hide the dogs' legs and feet. The hair is long, smooth, and straight. The hair on the head and legs is tan or gold. On the body and tail, it is steely blue. Some Yorkies have darker bodies than others.

The hair on Yorkies' heads is long, too. It sometimes covers the dogs' eyes. Many owners clip the hair around the eyes. Others pull it up into a ponytail. They tie it with a bow.

Yorkies have black noses and dark eyes. Their ears are pointed and stick up. But sometimes their ears are hidden under all that hair.

A high ponytail on a dog's head is called a "topknot." Other kinds of long-haired dogs wear topknots, too.

13

Small, Yet Smart and Brave

Yorkies are friendly, smart, and full of energy. They are sweet and loving to their owners. Sometimes they try too hard to **protect** them. They might growl and bark at strangers. They might try to keep their owners' friends away. They might try to keep other pets away. Yorkies will snap at dogs much bigger than they are. But Yorkies can learn, too. They quickly get used to new people and animals.

These two Yorkies are barking at a neighbor's dog. They are telling him to stay away from their yard!

Some people are glad their Yorkies bark at strangers. They feel safer with their little watchdogs around.

Yorkies are great pets for people who live alone. They are good for people in small homes. Yorkies like to go outside if they get the chance. But they can get plenty of exercise inside.

Some Yorkies can be stubborn. But most Yorkie owners say their dogs are great. These little dogs can learn lots of tricks. People teach them to jump through hoops. Others teach them to do "high fives."

Yorkies' size makes them easy to carry around. Some people hold the little dogs in their arms. Others carry their Yorkies around in purses, baskets, or even slings!

This dog's owner is carrying his Yorkie in a sling. This keeps the dog safe when visiting a crowded park.

Yorkshire Puppies

Yorkie mothers often have two or three puppies in a **litter**. Some litters have only one pup. Others have as many as five. The newborn puppies are black and tan. As they get older, they turn golden tan and steely blue.

Newborn Yorkies are tiny. They can fit in a child's hand. Like all newborn puppies, they are weak and helpless.

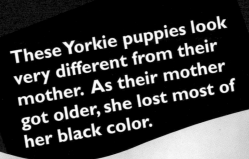
These Yorkie puppies look very different from their mother. As their mother got older, she lost most of her black color.

Their eyes are closed. Their ears cannot hear yet. But the puppies can feel things. They can feel their brothers and sisters nearby. They can feel when someone picks them up.

The puppies start growing right away. In about two weeks, they open their eyes. They move around more. By eight weeks, they can see and hear well. They are no longer helpless. They run around, wag their tails, and bark. They are still tiny, though. People need to treat them gently.

These first few weeks are important. The pups learn how to get along with other dogs. They learn how to get along with people. That makes them friendlier when someone takes them home.

These Yorkie puppies are about six weeks old.

Yorkies at Home and at Work

Many people keep Yorkies as pets. Some people put their Yorkies in dog shows. They **groom** their dogs so they look their best. They take very good care of them.

Some people teach their Yorkies to be **therapy** dogs. These dogs visit people who are ill. Being around animals can help sick people feel better. Yorkies are small enough to sit on peoples' laps. They cuddle with the people. They do tricks for them. They help the people feel better.

This little Yorkie is visiting a seniors' center. The people there are always happy to see him!

23

One Yorkie became famous for cheering up **soldiers**. The dog's name was Smoky. During World War Two, a soldier found her in the jungle. The year was 1944. The little dog was hungry and afraid. A soldier named Bill took Smoky in. He fed her and taught her tricks.

Smoky knew over 200 tricks. She also visited hospitals and children's homes for 10 years after the war. Smoky died in 1957.

Soon, Smoky was showing off for other soldiers. She knew some great tricks. She could even walk a tightrope! Bill trained Smoky to help the soldiers with very important jobs. Smoky learned to do dangerous jobs, too. She became a war hero! The soldiers grew to love the little terrier. Today, people remember her as Smoky the War Dog. In Ohio, there is a monument in her honor.

Smoky weighed just 4 pounds (2 kg). She could fit inside her owner's helmet!

Caring for a Yorkshire Terrier

Two things make Yorkshire terriers stand out. They are tiny, and they have long, beautiful coats. These same two things can cause some problems.

Tiny dogs can get hurt easily. Jumping down from chairs can hurt their legs. Yorkies are hard for people to see. People sometimes trip over them. Children might play roughly with them.

Some Yorkies can have trouble with their teeth. Regular checkups by a **veterinarian** can stop problems before they start.

26

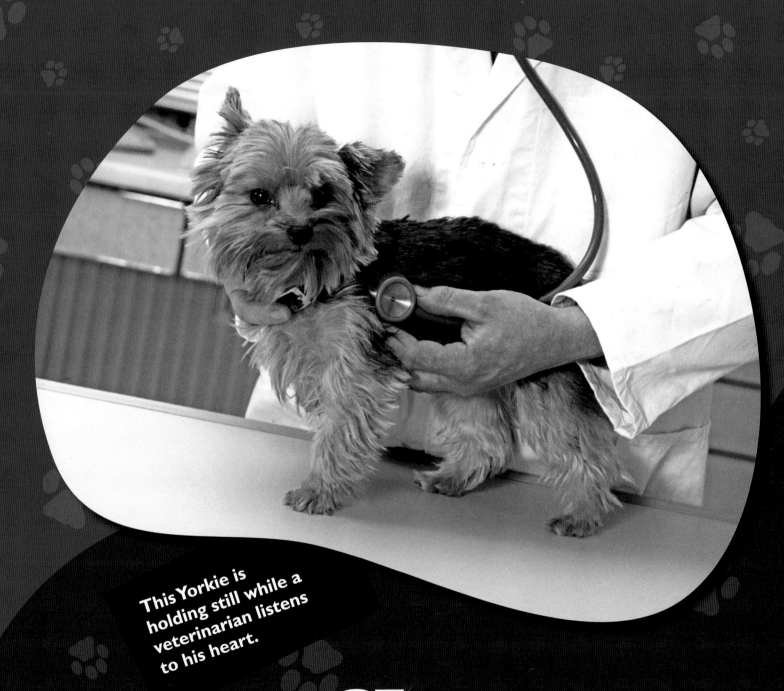

This Yorkie is holding still while a veterinarian listens to his heart.

Some Yorkies have problems with weak throats. Their throats can cave in, making it hard for them to breathe.

Bigger dogs might bite at them. All these things can hurt the dogs.

Yorkies need grooming. Their long hair should be brushed every day. The hair also picks up dirt. It needs to be washed often. Some owners cut their Yorkies' hair short. That makes it easier to care for. Even with their long coats, Yorkies get cold easily. They do not have a thick undercoat like many dogs. The undercoat keeps the other dogs warm. For Yorkies, wearing a coat or sweater can help.

Some Yorkies have knee or back problems. Their kneecaps or backbones can slip out of place. Jumping or playing roughly makes things worse.

Most people take good care of their Yorkshire terriers. They have their dogs for 10 or 15 years. These little dogs live long and happy lives.

This Yorkie has a short haircut. In cooler weather, her owner puts a sweater on her.

Glossary

breeds (BREEDZ) Breeds are certain types of an animal. Yorkshire terriers and poodles are two breeds of dogs.

groom (GROOM) When you groom an animal, you clean and brush it. Yorkies need to be groomed often.

litter (LIH-tur) A litter is a group of babies born to one animal. Yorkies often have two or three puppies in a litter.

popular (PAH-pyuh-lur) When something is popular, it is liked by lots of people. Yorkshire terriers are popular dogs.

protect (pruh-TEKT) To protect something is to keep it safe. Yorkies try to protect their owners.

soldiers (SOHL-jurz) Soldiers are people who are in the army. A Yorkie named Smoky helped soldiers in World War Two.

therapy (THER-uh-pee) Therapy is treatment for an illness or other problem. Visits from therapy dogs can make ill people feel better.

veterinarian (vet-rih-NAIR-ee-un) A veterinarian is a doctor who takes care of animals. Veterinarians are often called "vets" for short.

To Find Out More

Books to Read

American Kennel Club. *The Complete Dog Book for Kids.* New York: Howell Book House, 1996.

Downing, Elizabeth. *Guide to Owning a Yorkshire Terrier.* Philadelphia, PA: Chelsea House Publishers, 1995.

Gewirtz, Elaine Waldorf. *Your Yorkshire Terrier's Life: Your Complete Guide to Raising Your Pet from Puppy to Companion.* Roseville, CA: Prima Pets, 2000.

Gordon, Joan B. *The New Complete Yorkshire Terrier.* New York: Howell Book House, 1993.

Stone, Lynn M. *Yorkshire Terriers.* Vero Beach, FL: Rourke Publishing, 2005.

Places to Contact

American Kennel Club (AKC) Headquarters
260 Madison Ave, New York, NY 10016
Telephone: 212-696-8200

On the Web

Visit our Web site for lots of links about Yorkshire terriers:

http://www.childsworld.com/links

Note to Parents, Teachers, and Librarians: We routinely check our Web links to make sure they're safe, active sites—so encourage your readers to check them out!

Index

About the Author

Susan H. Gray has a Master's degree in zoology. She has written more than 70 science and reference books for children. She loves to garden and play the piano. Susan lives in Cabot, Arkansas, with her husband Michael and many pets.